Anger Management

Cease The Detrimental Impact On The Parent-child Bonding Prior To Its Irreversible Consequences: Strategies To Combat Anxiety, Coping With Daily Pressures, Regulating Emotional Responses,

Norberto Everett

TABLE OF CONTENT

Analyzing Emotions To Identify Resolutions 1

Think About Anger Management 13

Unearth The Underlying Cause Of Your Anger. 30

Anger And Substance Abuse 65

Effectively Managing Anger Through The Acquisition Of The Ability To Experience Annoyance. 90

Fundamental Factors That May Contribute To Challenges In Anger Management 109

Children Diagnosed With Attention Deficit Hyperactivity Disorder (Adhd) And Exhibiting Challenges In Regulating Their Anger. 140

Analyzing Emotions To Identify Resolutions

If you have been experiencing prolonged irritability without any evident cause, or perhaps due to a minor issue that does not warrant such a strong response, it would be advisable to allocate some time for introspection. Ideally, this would occur subsequent to the subsiding of your initial feelings of anger, leaving you with a persisting sense of vexation and exasperation. Consider the potential sources of your distress and analyze the matter systematically. Ideally, it would be prudent to document this information with the intention of gaining a more lucid comprehension of the subject matter at hand.

After identifying the particular matter that is causing you distress, your objective should be to refute it through the use of rationality. Bear in mind: the power of rationality outweighs the influence of wrath! As the latter tends to be predominantly irrational, seeking a logical rationale could potentially serve as the remedy you require. If you have been experiencing a persistent state of irritability following a disagreement with your spouse regarding insufficient time spent together, I encourage you to take a seat and commence the process of documenting the possible causes for this emotional state. Kindly assess whether both of you desire to allocate time with one another. In the event that your response is affirmative, kindly enumerate the underlying factors that contribute to the scarcity of your time. If each of you maintains different working hours, it serves as a legitimate indication for the underlying reason, thereby rendering any self-directed or spouse-directed anger irrational.

In a comparable fashion, should you ascertain that the root cause of your anger lies within diminished self-worth, and that your customary response to criticism involves adopting defensive mechanisms, employ rationality to refute self-deprecating thoughts. In the event of receiving workplace criticism, it is advisable to compile a comprehensive record of instances where one has been commended or valued. Subsequently, it is important to engage in reflective contemplation to discern the rationale behind the criticism at hand. Through the utilization of rational thinking and adopting a constructive mindset, it will become evident to you that your justifications for displaying aggression may lack merit in due course.

After arriving at rational justifications for a given situation, one may proceed to explore analogous resolutions. Approaching a problem in this manner, rather than persisting in a state of perpetual anger and negativity, will cultivate a framework for rationality within oneself. Over time, this will establish a beneficial pattern of behavior. Furthermore, documenting the underlying factors behind each instance of anger will enable you to discern recurring patterns and ascertain the primary catalysts for your emotional response.

Cognitive Restructuring

Cognitive processes encompass the mental faculties one engages in during various circumstances. To mitigate excessive contemplation and mitigate the instigation of anger in demanding circumstances, a pivotal approach entails restructuring cognitive processes. Although this may not provide immediate resolution, it is imperative that you consistently engage in this practice over an extended period in order to attain optimal outcomes. Through the passage of several months or years, one has the potential to cultivate a greater sense of calm both in their outward demeanor and cognitive state.

Embrace and cherish yourself - Despite the perceived intractability of halting the cascade of thoughts that inundate you during moments of frustration, it is imperative that you recognize your inner agency and the capacity to regulate your mind. Firstly, it is imperative to eliminate all the adverse emotions connected with anger. For instance, rather than affirming that "I possess an exceedingly aggressive demeanor and a severe issue, and my ability to exercise self-control is completely absent," consider reframing the problem with a more optimistic perspective. Convey to yourself, "I am faced with an issue, but I possess the capability to address it, and recognizing this truth is the initial stride towards my restoration."

Adopt an optimistic perspective - The most effective approach to reconfigure your cognitive processes is to examine small details and elements that prompt you to engage in exaggerated thinking. As an illustration, endeavor to recollect your thoughts during a conflict with your spouse. Instead of thinking, "We always end up fighting; this is a horrible relationship," remind yourself of the times that you do not fight. It can be exceedingly challenging to perceive the positive aspects of situations when one experiences anger, and this is precisely the lesson that needs to be grasped.

Exercise control over your choice of words - Keep in mind that the language you employ, both aloud and mentally, can significantly impact your emotional state. Commence the practice of omitting overly exaggerated language from your lexicon. As an illustration, it is advised to refrain from employing absolute terms such as "never" and "always." Avoid forming conclusions such as "My superior always criticizes me" or "My spouse never comprehends my emotions." Instead, opt for more moderate vocabulary that accurately represents the typical level of intensity. The most effective approach would be to commence the process by carefully monitoring your language and making conscious efforts to regulate your vocabulary. Over time, this assimilation will become ingrained in your cognitive processes, too.

Meditation

When your aggression exerts dominance over all aspects of your existence, it is unrealistic to anticipate its dissolution through the mere application of relaxation techniques during episodes of fury. If you possess profound tendencies of aggression, it will become imperative for you to gradually introduce incremental modifications to your overall way of life, regardless of the instances in which you experience feelings of anger. Meditation stands as an exemplary manifestation of these constructive and beneficial transformations. It has been observed to induce a state of tranquility in individuals and can serve as a significant means for introspection and self-discovery.

Frequently, feelings of frustration arise due to excessive engagement in the daily rigors of life, which leaves little opportunity to allocate time for mental revitalization. Conversely, you persist in engaging in a demanding regimen on a daily basis, thereby burdening your mental serenity in the process. Allocating a period for meditative practice can provide an effective means to restore one's inner connection, while concurrently revitalizing the cognitive resources required to manage everyday responsibilities. Undoubtedly, when you embark on your workday with a sense of tranquility and contentment, the minor actions of others will have less capacity to incite irritation within you.

The manner in which you choose to engage in meditation is entirely at your discretion. Whether you opt for engaging in morning yoga or allotting a dedicated period for introspection accompanied by employing self-empowering discourse, it is imperative that you prioritize the act of relinquishing detrimental energy and replacing it with a state of tranquility.

- Last but not least, make sure to place your trust in the individuals who comprise your social circle. Individuals who experience anger often exhibit cynicism and encounter difficulty in placing trust in others. Truly speaking, if the individuals in your life have remained steadfast despite your proclivity for anger, it is likely that they merit your trust.

- In ninth place, strive to cultivate active listening skills. In moments of anger, your attention becomes selective and you solely perceive what aligns with your desires. It is imperative that you exert conscious effort to cease all activity and attentively engage with the individual communicating with you. It is advisable to recapitulate their statements to ensure absolute clarity regarding your attentive reception of their message. It is essential that you actively participate in the discussion instead of expending your energy on negative emotions and attempting to develop a retort throughout the entire conversation. Just listen!

• Tenth - demonstrate confidence and self-assurance while maintaining respectful communication. A person exhibiting aggressive behavior can be likened to a forceful bulldozer, imposing their opinions and emotions onto others. A person who possesses a confident demeanor is capable of effectively articulating their thoughts in a manner that upholds courtesy.

• Lastly, bear in mind the importance of forgiving and letting go. Maintaining long-lasting resentment is not advantageous when it comes to effectively managing one's anger. Harboring resentment enables the simmering and insidious growth of anger within you, ultimately resulting in the alienation of others who will come to dread the relentless rehashing of their past errors. One must cultivate the ability to pardon errors: deliberately release them from memory, and subsequently progress forward. The ability to pardon and disregard transgressions is a pivotal asset in effectively handling one's anger.

These instruments will provide you with a strong basis and enable you to effectively enhance your understanding of and handle your anger. Practice them daily!

Think About Anger Management

One highly effective approach is to acquire strategies for effectively managing one's anger. For certain individuals, it may be necessary to enlist the assistance of a professional and participate in anger management sessions in order to effectively regulate and manage one's emotions. For individuals seeking alternative approaches, it may be beneficial to experiment with some of the strategies discussed in the subsequent sections of this guidebook, with the aim of achieving desired outcomes.

If you find yourself in the nascent phases of managing your anger, you can confidently experiment with the recommendations delineated in this instructional manual. Detaching oneself from the situation, engaging in written reflection, and seeking a confidante to discuss the matter can prove to be effective strategies for effectively managing and mitigating the presence of anger.

Conversely, should you find yourself contending with persistent underlying anger that relentlessly lingers, it may be prudent to consider elevating the response level accordingly. The anger management classes, in conjunction with the assistance of a qualified professional, can assist you in identifying the underlying source of your anger and facilitate the development of strategies to manage it in a manner that is both secure and efficacious.

No individual desires to establish a reputation as an irate individual lacking the ability to maintain emotional composure. It is imperative to promptly identify the indicators of anger in order to assume command over one's emotions and prevent them from exerting control.

Guideline 1: Utilize Periods of Rest

The initial suggestion that we will examine is to engage in a period of rest or relaxation. When you begin to sense that your anger is becoming uncontrollable and may lead to an outburst, it is advisable to temporarily disengage from the task at hand. If it is feasible, it would be advisable for you to also endeavor to remove yourself from the entity or situation that is chiefly causing distress. This serves as an optimal method to enable oneself to distance from that trigger and effectively achieve a state of calmness. It additionally serves to redirect your focus from the source of your initial distress.

There are numerous means by which you can avail yourself of respite and disengage from your responsibilities. The course of action you pursue will be contingent upon the specific circumstances you find yourself confronted with. There are several instances in which you can effectively utilize this approach, as illustrated by the subsequent examples:

Dealing with road rage? It is imperative to promptly locate a secure location in order to bring the vehicle to a stop. Please switch off the vehicle's engine and allocate a brief moment to engage in deep breathing exercises in order to restore a sense of well-being.

Feeling angry at work? If it is feasible for you to take a respite, this might be an opportune moment to do so. Kindly venture outside unaccompanied, to a serene and tranquil location, or alternatively, seek solace in an unoccupied chamber, should one be available. You might additionally contemplate stepping out to the vehicle and partaking in a few minutes of radio-listening to relax.

Are you experiencing any feelings of anger while in the comfort of your residence? One can still find means of escapism even in the confines of one's own dwelling. If one is engaged in the care of youngsters and cannot readily leave the premises, it may be prudent to retreat to a private space such as one's chamber or a restroom, discreetly shutting the door for a brief interval. Alternatively, if feasible, contemplate taking a serene stroll to ameliorate the situation.

Experiencing anger in an unfamiliar environment? It is advisable to refrain from embarking on solitary walks. Inform the individual accompanying you to that location of your desire to embark upon a temporary cessation. They have the option to accompany you, at which point you can attain the serene ambiance you desire.

There may arise occasions wherein we experience frustration or resentment towards the prevailing circumstances surrounding us. On occasion, a strategic retreat and temporary respite from the circumstances can engender a notable improvement in one's well-being.

4. Recognize your inherent uniqueness and value.

Individuals who experience persistent anger tend to feel disheartened when they perceive themselves in a less favorable light than their peers. They may inwardly remark, 'Behold Bob and Jennifer.' They consistently exhibit a calm demeanor and rarely display signs of anger. I must acknowledge that my behavior has been uncultivated and lacking in maturity.

It is inadvisable to draw comparisons between your own vulnerabilities and the strengths of others. This can be likened to contrasting your collection of outtakes with their compilation of notable achievements. When confronted with an unavoidable shortfall, you will succumb to the ensnarement of self-critique.

Self-compassion prompts individuals to adopt an alternative viewpoint when assessing their own actions. It facilitates the recognition that irrespective of one's level of performance, each individual possesses inherent worthiness and thus, is deserving of cultivating self-love and embracing oneself.

Based on firsthand experience, I understand the immense challenge one faces in accepting and embracing this reality. For an excessive number of years, my sense of value and self-esteem relied exclusively on my immediate performance. My self-esteem perpetually fluctuated in accordance with my most recent achievements or shortcomings. Fortunately, I began to realize my inherent value and worth, apart from my performance. This aided in preventing me from succumbing to self-reproach whenever I did not exercise restraint over my emotions.

Acquire the ability to cherish oneself, display kindness towards oneself, and extend self-forgiveness, as it is only through cultivating a positive disposition towards oneself that we can develop the proper disposition towards others.

-Wilfred Peterson

5. Practice Self-forgiveness

A significant component of self-compassion lies in the propensity to readily extend forgiveness to oneself, in instances where errors are made or standards are not met. Self-absolution facilitates the resolution of any remorse or dishonor that may be stemming from your episode of anger.

If you are unwilling to grant yourself forgiveness, you may find yourself immersed in self-condemnation. This has the potential to result in the onset of depression or, at the very least, a negative emotional state, both of which could contribute to the intensification of your anger. Years ago, I encountered a situation where I would occasionally become irate during my interactions with my children. I persevered in self-criticism and harbored negative emotions until I reached a point where I deemed myself sufficiently disciplined and thoroughly educated from the experience.

Despite my desire to alter this detrimental practice, I found myself trapped in a recurring cycle. Upon developing awareness of the consequences stemming from my conduct, it became evident that I subjected myself to self-criticism subsequent to experiencing fits of anger or engaging in excessively severe interactions with others. I would permit my pessimistic thoughts and remorse to accumulate to such an extent that I ceased my efforts in addressing and controlling my anger.

I dedicated considerable time to reproaching myself for my offensive actions, thereby neglecting to perceive forthcoming interactions as a chance to rectify my conduct. Similar to numerous individuals who contend with fits of anger, I possessed minimal, if any, inclination towards self-compassion. Luckily, I happened upon a poignant quote that aided me in disrupting the deleterious pattern.

The quote is commonly ascribed to Albert Einstein, although its true origin can be traced back to a twelve-step support program known as Narcotics Anonymous. This erroneous pattern of behavior I engaged in involved consistently repeating the same actions while harbouring the irrational expectation of obtaining disparate outcomes. On every occasion that I fell below expectations, I subjected myself to feelings of remorse and self-denial. I thought that this would motivate me to do better next time. Due to the ineffectiveness of my present approach, I opted to pursue an alternative course of action.

I recalled an additional quotation from a notable figure whom I hold in high regard, C.S. Lewis, the esteemed author of The Chronicles of Narnia and other renowned literary works. He expressed his belief that in the event of receiving forgiveness from God, it becomes imperative for us to extend forgiveness to ourselves. Otherwise, we would be assuming a position of superiority over Him, which is not appropriate. Recognizing God's boundless love and mercy, I made a conscious decision to extend forgiveness to myself and cultivate a mindset of self-compassion. To my astonishment, my innovative approach facilitated a rejuvenation of my endeavors.

The findings derived from my experimental attempts have been validated through the scrutiny of empirical investigations. A research endeavor led by Timothy Pychyl, Ph.D. at Carleton University investigated the potential impact of self-forgiveness on enhancing academic performance in subsequent examinations. Individuals who granted themselves lenience for their failure to engage in academic preparation for an examination were able to commence anew.

One instance of practicing self-compassion has the potential to significantly alter the course of your entire day. A succession of such moments possesses the potential to significantly alter the trajectory of one's life.

-Christopher Germer

In the case of individuals who practiced self-forgiveness, their dedication to studying for the subsequent test showed a notable increase of 25 percent, resulting in higher academic performance, as opposed to those who did not grant themselves forgiveness. This facilitated an enhancement in their performance in contrast to students who persisted in self-criticism.

As previously stated, the act of practicing self-forgiveness does not revolve around engaging in self-gratification. It entails a sincere recognition and admission of one's error, exemplified by the occurrence of an emotionally charged outburst. However, the error does not need to dictate or characterize you as an individual or your future behaviors.

Self-forgiveness additionally entails acknowledging precisely how one could have averted the error or enhanced one's performance. After you have identified and established the changes you will make in future instances, you can proceed with granting yourself forgiveness. The expeditiousness with which you are capable of pardoning yourself and cultivating self-compassion will greatly facilitate the process of advancing.

6. Self-soothe

Throughout the duration of my battle with chronic anger, I observed that once my temper was lost, achieving a state of calm proved to be a formidable task. The perpetuation of my pessimistic state of mind heightened my sensitivity towards factors that instigated my anger. I came to the realization that it was imperative for me to discover a means of liberating myself from the negative spiral and enhancing my emotional state.

Fortunately, through extensive research on the subject of self-compassion, I fortuitously encountered a beneficial methodology known as self-soothing. This entails utilizing one or multiple senses to achieve a state of calm and tranquility. Self-regulatory strategies can be employed during times of anger or following a mistake, in order to impede the ceaseless flow of self-deprecating thoughts. Moreover, in addition to its benefits, engaging in self-soothing techniques can effectively alleviate stress levels, thereby enabling better regulation of one's temper.

Unearth The Underlying Cause Of Your Anger.

1. Reflect upon whether you have experienced any form of harm or injury.

There are numerous manifestations in which anger can arise from emotional pain. A potentially unrestrained altercation could have escalated, leading to the utterance of regrettable remarks. It is possible that you have experienced betrayal, or that you have been subjected to physical discomfort. Irrespective of the underlying reason, discomfort is undesired by both the physical and emotional self, leading the afflicted individual to potentially react with aggression. This is how pain is converted into anger as a mechanism for coping. As a manifestation of the innate drive for survival in humans, anger serves as a catalyst for taking action, reestablishing equilibrium, and ultimately eradicating the origin of distress.

2. Identify the Reason Behind Your Fear

Unfamiliarity often elicits trepidation, and apprehension concerning potential outcomes can evolve into hostility. This phenomenon occurs when there is a lack of comprehensive comprehension surrounding the movement or alteration of an entity in an unpredictable manner. This situation can also arise when an individual faces the dilemma of either accepting their lack of knowledge or harboring resentment towards their own inability to comprehend it. Occasionally, surrendering to the emotion and avoiding the inclination to strategize a more effective method to overcome fear may seem preferable. The genesis of anger stems from the realm of the unfamiliar, where alternative responses become arduous, if not unattainable.

3. Examine the Origin of Your Regret

The manifestation of anger directed towards oneself often arises from feelings of guilt. In the event that you have expressed or engaged in an action that you deem to be highly regrettable, it is possible for feelings of guilt to arise, even after the matter has been successfully addressed. This could potentially stem from a perception that you have not faced sufficient repercussions. As a form of self-retribution, you may find yourself experiencing a sense of anger towards your own actions. This type of anger poses a formidable challenge due to its intrinsic characteristics. To attain release from this burden, it will be necessary to revisit the root cause of guilt; the previously mended emotional injuries may require being reopened so as to address the lingering unresolved matter that was previously suppressed.

4. Contemplate the Causes of Your Envy

When an individual acquires something desirable that you covet, feelings of envy will manifest themselves. It is possible that you perceive yourself as more deserving of the object bestowed upon the individual, surpassing their capacity to appreciate its value. Envy may also arise from circumstances in which one desires to be selected, yet has been overlooked. There is consistently an inherent belief in one's entitlement to that particular item or preference over the alternative. This starkly contrasts with the mere desire of acquiring something unattainable due to factors like distance, time, or limited resources, which is further complicated by the involvement of another individual. Once your uncontrolled envy takes hold, that individual could potentially become the recipient of your anger.

5. Acquire a comprehensive understanding of the grounds for your denial

If you have arrived to present something, it is likely that you have devoted significant effort to the development of that artifact, concept, or proposition. Considerable time, effort, and potentially even financial resources have been dedicated to the development of the proposition at hand, whether it be a gift, a project idea, a proposal for a relationship, or a mere conversation. Above all, it was imperative that your level of confidence be significantly improved prior to subjecting yourself to evaluation. The experience of rejection will inevitably lead to the ensuing emotional anguish. In the event that the explanation provided is inadequate or difficult to be accepted, it is plausible that a sense of being neglected might arise, subsequently giving rise to feelings of anger.

Strategies for immediately managing and regulating feelings of anger

One possible alternative in a formal tone could be: "A viable approach to managing anger entails removing oneself from a provocative circumstance." In instances where discussions become intense, it is advisable to pause and withdraw temporarily. Leave the place entirely. In the event that you are experiencing emotional distress due to the behavior of your children, I recommend taking a leisurely stroll. Taking a brief respite can play a crucial role in assisting you with soothing both your mental faculties and physical state.

If there is an individual with whom you frequently engage in confrontational disputes, it is advisable to discuss with them the significance of taking a break and recommencing the discussion when both parties are in a composed state.

When you find it necessary to temporarily disengage, kindly clarify that you are not attempting to evade challenging matters, but rather focusing on effectively managing your anger.

ENGAGE IN CONVERSATION WITH AN ACQUAINTANCE

Engaging in discussion or confiding in a confidante who possesses a soothing presence can prove highly advantageous when seeking resolution or emotional catharsis. However, it is crucial to acknowledge that the act of venting has the potential to yield adverse consequences. If you wish to engage in a conversation with a friend, it is imperative that you direct your efforts towards mutually devising a solution or mitigating your resentment, rather than merely expressing personal frustrations. It is unjust to rely on them as your primary source of advice. Utilizing this approach effectively entails focusing on an aspect unrelated to the inciting situation that elicits anger.

GET MOVING

Anger elicits a surge of heightened vitality. Engaging in physical activity is considered as one of the most effective exercises for anger management. Whether you go for a brisk walk or hit the gym, working out can burn off extra tension.

Engaging in regular physical activity also aids in alleviating stress and tension. It is possible that following an extended period of running or a strenuous exercise session, you might experience an enhanced clarity in perceiving and comprehending the matters that had previously been distressing to you.

MANAGE YOU THOUGHTS

Negative thoughts contribute to the exacerbation of anger. Ideations such as "I find it intolerable." This congestion on the road is likely to negatively impact all our plans and significantly contribute to augmenting your level of frustration. When confronted with thoughts that ignite anger within you, consider reframing your mindset. Instead, consider contemplating notions such as "There exists a vast multitude of vehicles traversing the roads daily." Occasionally, traffic congestion may occur. Furthermore, it may be beneficial to cultivate a personal mantra, which can be recited as a means to suppress the thoughts that contribute to your anger. Expressing statements such as "I am alright" or "I am doing fine." Repeatedly maintaining a composed demeanor and refraining from unproductive reactions can facilitate the reduction of hostile cognitions.

FOCUS ON RELAXATION

There are numerous anger management techniques entailing relaxation. It is imperative to locate the method that is most effective for your needs. Breath control techniques and the practice of progressive muscle relaxation are two frequently employed methods for alleviating tension. Both exercises can be executed expeditiously and inconspicuously. It is essential to acknowledge, nonetheless, that relaxation exercises require practice. Initially, one may perceive them to be ineffectual, or harbor doubts regarding their suitability for one's needs. However, through diligent practice, these techniques can evolve into your preferred approaches to effectively manage feelings of anger.

EXPLORE YOUR FEELINGS

Occasionally, it can be beneficial to pause and reflect upon the underlying emotions that may be accompanying your anger. Anger frequently assumes a defensive guise in order to shield oneself from experiencing more agonizing sentiments such as humiliation, melancholy, and frustration.

In cases where an individual receives unwanted feedback, it is possible for them to react by directing their frustrations towards the source owing to feelings of embarrassment. One might argue that by attributing negative intentions to the person criticizing you, you are merely trying to shield yourself from feelings of embarrassment. Recognizing the inherent emotions can facilitate an exploration of the fundamental causes, thereby enabling informed decision-making and subsequent intervention.

Refrain from repressing or inhibiting your anger.

Identifying the root cause of your anger yields greater efficacy than repressing it. Whilst it may be alluring to attempt to diminish an unfavorable emotion, the act of completely denying your anger is likely to engender heightened levels of stress.

ESTABLISH A 'RELAXATION' KIT

In the event that one typically arrives home from work burdened and subsequently vents anger upon their family, or if workplace meetings consistently provoke substantial frustration, it is advisable to establish a designated relaxation kit to help restore tranquility. Consider items that facilitate the stimulation of all your senses. By engaging your senses to observe, listen to, perceive, detect, and physically experience soothing stimuli, you can effectively alter your emotional condition. A relaxation toolkit could potentially encompass fragrant hand lotion, a depiction of a tranquil scenery, a contemplative excerpt suitable for recitation, or a select few indulgent sweets. Incorporate elements that you are aware will facilitate your ability to maintain a state of tranquility.

It may be prudent for you to consider establishing a portable virtual relaxation kit that can be conveniently carried along. These are resources that can be summoned as required and possess greater mobility. For example, serene musical compositions and soothing visuals, accompanied by expertly-guided meditation or detailed prompts for controlled respiration techniques, may be conveniently organized within a designated directory on your mobile device.

The majority of individuals have experienced a state of emotional disruption during a significant altercation within their family or while encountering severe traffic congestion during their commute to work. Despite the discomfort it brings, anger can serve as a catalyst for driving constructive change in areas of our lives that are not functioning optimally, such as resolving relationship conflicts or addressing uncomfortable work circumstances.

However, anger is a potent sentiment that, if allowed to go unchecked, has the potential to give rise to feelings of discontent and even contribute to the development of a mental health disorder. Additionally, it has the potential to induce irrational or hostile behavior. This may lead to the consequences of social isolation, adverse health outcomes, and instances of abuse.

A significant number of individuals are more prone to experiencing anger compared to others. Individuals experiencing high levels of distress may encounter challenges in managing their ire. A study conducted by researchers revealed that individuals who suffer from mental health disorders in their childhood or experience traumatic brain injuries as adults exhibit a greater propensity towards experiencing intense anger.

Fortunately, there are available resources and this book is among them. Research indicates that engagement in anger management exercises has demonstrated enhanced overall welfare and a decrease in the frequency of hostile outbursts within these vulnerable populations. If you encounter difficulties in pacifying your anger, these exercises may also provide assistance.

7: Journaling

Throughout the course of history, the practice of journaling has been widely acknowledged and utilized as a valuable instrument for individuals of artistic and intellectual prowess. Due to its emphasis on the intellect and its facilitation of goal-setting, it has been observed that numerous luminaries in the realms of science and the arts engaged in the practice of maintaining journals. A number of these works have been disseminated through publication channels, while a portion of them continues to be exhibited within museum settings. Upon perusing these journals, one comes to comprehend not merely the intellectual acumen of the authors but also their strikingly typical nature. The composition of these journals differs among writers, as some individuals adhere to a conventional structure of handwritten entries, while others capture and document spontaneous thoughts and illustrations that require a suitable medium for their existence.

Distinguished physicist Albert Einstein curated journals that meticulously documented his expeditions, his scientific postulations, and an extensive collection of lecture notes numbering in the tens of thousands. Marie Curie, the prominent figure behind the uncovering of radioactivity, maintained her research records within her journals, which endured such extensive exposure to radiation that they necessitate preservation within lead storage containers for thousands of years. The colorful yet sorrowful journal of Frida Kahlo encompasses vivid illustrations portraying the artist's life, documenting her waning health and interconnectedness with others. In the realm of profound intellects, Leonardo da Vinci stands as an exemplar who documented his groundbreaking scientific theories through a series of esteemed journals. These illustrious manuscripts not only contained captivating illustrations that depicted his pioneering concepts but also juxtaposed seemingly trivial aspects of daily life, such as grocery lists, with dexterously rendered sketches and intricate thoughts of paramount significance. Each of these illustrations serves as evidence that the act of journaling is entirely dependent on one's personal approach, and there exists no singular method of maintaining a journal.

Attaining objectives: For further elaboration, with reference to the meal plan or food journal provided, at what time do you intend to consume your meals? What amount of preparation will you undertake beforehand? May I inquire about the specific time and duration of your intended physical exercise regimen? Alternatively, in relation to the illustration of the ambitious individual striving for a PhD, it would be prudent to consider the financial implications of pursuing this degree, the duration of the program, the anticipated post-graduation income, and the number of additional part-time work hours required to finance undergraduate studies. It is entirely within your discretion to obtain comprehensive information or not. However, increasing the level of detail enhances organizational precision and facilitates the development of intricate strategies.

There is no need for excessive concern regarding self-micromanagement, as the sole individual who will bear the responsibility for it shall be oneself. Having a multitude of plans with a comprehensive level of details is frequently more advantageous than relying on a singular plan with limited details. Let us reflect upon the aforementioned instances of journals: would the individual aiming to lose weight be adequately prepared for accomplishment if they neglected to meticulously review their initial few journal entries? What about the student? Failing to devise a coherent plan bears the inevitable consequence of failure. It is inconceivable as to why any rational individual would purposely orchestrate their own downfall.

Facilitating a path to achieve favorable outcomes need not entail complexity, but rather necessitates deliberate contemplation. Jotting down those thoughts for the purpose of analysis is an effective means of arranging and structuring them. Employ various visual aids such as graphs, lists, charts, paragraphs, drawings, and bullet points to effectively accomplish the task at hand. Ensure that you utilize every available resource and technique from your repertoire. Upon concluding this book, your repertoire will contain an array of novel concepts and approaches, thereby eliminating any justifications for neglecting the act of planning.

Rage and hostility exhibit synonymous characteristics.

Many individuals appear to mistakenly conflate the emotions of anger and aggressive conduct. Expressing anger in a constructive manner is beneficial, whereas resorting to aggressive conduct is not advisable. One can effectively manage anger in a healthful manner without engaging in any form of aggression. Aggression is never desirable.

The endeavor to manage one's anger is ultimately unavailing.

When individuals lack the requisite proficiency for regulating their anger, their emotions have the potential to unleash chaos upon their lives. Maladaptive manifestations of anger have the potential to not only engender difficulties within one's personal sphere, but can also impede one's professional endeavors. Therapeutic intervention, in conjunction with anger management techniques, can be highly beneficial in mitigating episodes of aggression. The efficacy of anger management should not be underestimated, as perceiving it as futile is merely a fallacy.

The situation exists solely within your mind.

Once again, it is a fallacy to assume that anger solely resides within one's consciousness. Please pause and reflect upon your most recent experience of intense anger. It is possible that you have encountered an elevation in your heart rate, perceived a sensation of facial warmth, and potentially experienced tremors in your hands. Therefore, it can be concluded that anger is not solely a psychological phenomenon, but rather a physiological reaction. Your body's physiological response tends to fuel your aggressive behavior, as well as angry thoughts. Through acquiring the skill of bodily relaxation, one can effectively alleviate mental tension, ultimately culminating in a state of tranquility. In order to effectively manage your anger, it is imperative to not only calm your mind but also induce relaxation in your physical state.

The release of anger occurs through the act of expressing it.

It is commonly held belief that expressing one's emotions through raised voice, engaging in aggressive actions towards inanimate objects or self-contained activities such as hitting a pillow, and potentially causing damage to one's surroundings can contribute to an improved sense of well-being. It is commonly understood that this practice can be beneficial as it provides an outlet for releasing accumulated anger. Nevertheless, these factors will merely exacerbate your negative emotions. To effectively manage and regulate your anger, it is imperative to gain a comprehensive understanding of its underlying causes. If one is unable to discern the root cause of the anger, then one shall perpetually struggle to address it. Therefore, the notion that expressing anger through outbursts or venting can effectively alleviate one's emotional state is unsubstantiated.

Disregard it, and it will dissipate.

Many individuals appear to believe that they can disregard their anger, with the expectation that it will dissipate over time. If you are attempting to restrain your anger, you are not behaving in a manner that benefits you. Repressing one's anger can have detrimental effects on one's well-being. Refrain from concealing your frustration through smiles, invalidating any feelings of anger you experience, or tolerating unjust treatment from others in order to evade confrontation. Refraining from expressing your anger and internally containing it will inevitably result in an eventual eruption of resentment. As previously indicated, repressing one's anger will inevitably lead to both physical and psychological afflictions. Suppressed anger has the potential to negatively impact cardiac well-being, exacerbate emotional state, and give rise to enduring feelings of animosity.

By dispelling these misconceptions, one can alter their perspective towards anger. Engaging in this activity constitutes the initial measure towards cultivating a constructive rapport with one's anger.

4: Utilizing Progressive Muscle Relaxation Techniques for Anger Management

In the preceding chapter, a session of deep breathing was engaged in as an exercise for inducing relaxation. In the following chapter, we will engage in the practice of progressive muscle relaxation. Engage in the exercise with regularity. Typically, anger tends to manifest through the physical manifestation of muscle tension. This tension builds up throughout your entire body and persists long after your anger has subsided. Progressive muscle relaxation induces relaxation throughout your entire body and aids in anger management.

Progressive Muscle Relaxation

Progressive muscle relaxation involves the deliberate contraction and subsequent release of specific muscle groups in the body. Through the utilization of this methodology, one will acquire the knowledge of discerning the distinct sensations associated with muscular tension and relaxation within each specific group of muscles. Through diligent practice, one shall acquire the ability to alleviate any undesirable tension (anger) that manifests throughout the entirety of one's physical being. Commence by initially targeting a considerable array of muscular groups, subsequently diminishing their count, thereby ensuring a condensed and transportable progressive relaxation technique. The subsequent diagram illustrates the primary muscle groups and presents suggestions for effectively contracting them.

Twelve muscular groupings: recommendations for muscle tensioning.

Forearm: Maintain a downward palm orientation, form a closed hand, and flex the wrist inward towards the upper arm.

Upper arm: Maintain your arms in close proximity to your body, contract your biceps, and draw the upper arm towards the lateral side. Allow the lower arm to dangle in a relaxed manner.

Extend the toes towards the knees, encompassing the lower leg and foot region.

Thighs: Exert force by firmly pressing your feet against the floor.

Abdomen: Retract your abdominal muscles posteriorly.

Respiration and Thoracic Region: Inhale gradually and deeply, maintaining the breath for a period of 10 seconds, subsequently allowing for relaxation.

Shoulders and lower neck: Elevate and retract your shoulders by performing a shrugging motion, subsequently drawing them upwards towards your ears.

Position the back of your head firmly against the chair's backrest.

Mouth: Gently bring your lips together, ensuring not to tightly close your teeth or jaw.

Eyes: Gently shut your eyes, ensuring not to exert excessive pressure.

Lowering the position of your forehead: Draw your eyebrows downwards.

Forehead region: Elevate the eyebrows, followed by crinkling of the forehead.

For the purpose of practicing, proceed to a tranquil space and assume a comfortable seated position on a chair. Prepare yourself by gradually easing into a more relaxed and comfortable position in the chair. Take deep, slow breaths. With each exhalation, visualize a gradual release of tension from your body, akin to the graceful departure of a bird in flight. Please shut your eyes and maintain a calm and steady breathing pattern. You may choose to keep your eyes open if doing so brings you comfort. Direct your attention to a singular point on the wall or floor. Once you have achieved a state of tranquility and are able to engage in profound focus, you are prepared to commence your physical exertions. Please maintain a regular rhythm of respiration while sequentially contracting and releasing every muscle group. Avoid holding your breath.

Tense

Commence by focusing on your hands and forearms. Breathe in, make fists and tense your lower arms and hands. Apply approximately 75% of the maximum tension to your hands. The degree of tension should be sufficient to elicit a taut sensation in your muscles, but it should not reach a level of pain.

Isolate

Make an effort to confine or contain the tension within a specific area to the greatest extent possible. The cruciality of effectively isolating one's tension cannot be overstated. Therefore, during the act of tensing your muscles, it would be beneficial to conduct a swift cognitive assessment to ascertain that neighboring muscles are not undergoing tension as well. For example, when one deliberately tenses the muscles in the lower arms and hands, the resulting tension should be confined solely to those specific regions. Initially, it is probable that you will also experience tension in various other regions of your physique, encompassing your lower limbs, abdominal region, upper torso, and even your respiration may cease. If you happen to observe this occurrence, endeavor to induce a state of calmness across all segments of your physique, excluding solely the specific muscular region which you intend to contract. Maintain a consistent and regular tempo of respiration.

Concentrate

Maintain a steady and regular pattern of respiration. Direct your attention to the sensation experienced in your arms and hands while you engage in the act of inhaling and exhaling. Maintain the tension for a duration of 2 to 3 breaths, approximately 10 to 15 seconds.

Flop

On the subsequent exhalation, release the tension and rapidly induce muscle relaxation. Envision a scenario where your muscles have experienced a loss of tension, akin to a rubber band when it is released. Direct your attention to the sensation of tranquility and observe the contrasting sensations between muscles in a state of relaxation and those held in tension. Maintain a regular breathing pattern, and after approximately three breaths, your muscles should attain a state of complete looseness and relaxation. Now you may proceed to initiate the process once more utilizing the same musculature.

Delegate the responsibility for the desire for retribution.

An alternative approach to curbing the tendency to blame others is to employ the practice of "responsibility transfer" as a means of seeking retribution. This can be achieved by reminding oneself that the dispensation of retribution and fairness lies beyond individual control. You are delegating the responsibility for these two to a higher authority. The majority of individuals implore for equity, while some opt to allow the legal proceedings to progress.

Imbalanced life

Certain individuals are experiencing discontentment due to the absence of equilibrium in their daily existence. They toil throughout the day without any chance to relax. They are unable to derive satisfaction from the modest joys in life. They lack a valid justification for experiencing joy and optimism. Their lives are characterized by a surplus of negative circumstances and a dearth, or even absence, of positive ones.

Insufficient provision of a network for managing anger

We, as individuals, exhibit inherent social tendencies. We cannot function alone. Even individuals with the most introverted tendencies recognize the significance of love, companionship, and social support. The majority of individuals rely on their families as a source of emotional support. In the presence of negative emotions, we consistently have access to a compassionate confidant who attentively lends an ear and occasionally imparts guidance to ameliorate our distress.

Certain individuals lack access to such a support network. Immigrants in a particular nation, for instance, often experience a sense of seclusion due to a lack of access to a support network. Similarly, this applies to individuals who are marginalized or excluded in educational institutions and professional settings. They lack individuals to confide in when they simply require a sympathetic ear.

In the event that you find yourself facing such circumstances in life, it is imperative that you refrain from yielding to anger due to this very rationale. You consistently possess the opportunity to engage in conversation with another individual. Should you possess a hobby, it behooves you to seek out a prospective companion who shares the same hobby. In the present day, we are afforded the opportunity to leverage the internet as a cost-effective means of communication, thereby enabling us to access and connect with our support networks.

Extreme levels of stress

Individuals who experience significantly heightened levels of stress are susceptible to developing a propensity for anger. Not all varieties of stress give rise to feelings of anger. The majority of individuals are capable of managing various types of stress both at their workplace and in their personal lives. Nevertheless, should these stressors persist, they have the potential to provoke anger within an individual. Upon the initial encounter with a stressor, an individual has the potential to effectively relinquish its effects. Gradually, however, we begin to grow weary of that particular source of stress. If the aforementioned stressor is not eliminated, it has the potential to overpower our emotional state and incite overwhelming anger.

Anger And Substance Abuse

Throughout substance abuse intervention, anger has consistently served as a notable contributing factor. Regrettably, until a recent point in time, it had been disregarded or regarded as an incidental consideration by substance abuse programs throughout the nation.

The utilization and misapplication of substances frequently coexist with irate emotions, hostile conduct, and violence inflicted upon oneself or others. According to the findings of the National Household Survey on Drug Abuse conducted by the Substance Abuse and Mental Health Administration, it was revealed that 40% of individuals who frequently use cocaine admitted to partaking in acts of violence or displaying aggressive behavior.

The presence of anger and aggression frequently plays a causal role in the initiation of drug and alcohol usage, while also serving as a consequence commonly linked to substance abuse. Individuals who are subjected to distressing occurrences frequently manifest anger and engage in violent behavior, in addition to resorting to substance abuse as a means of coping.

The prevalence of substance abuse and dependency has exceeded even the most pessimistic projections from previous years. In the United States alone, approximately 23 million individuals are contending on a daily basis with various manifestations of substance abuse or dependency.

The societal impact manifests significantly when considering the proportion of families experiencing the repercussion of cohabitating with an individual grappling with addiction, exemplified by:

Job loss,

Incarceration,

Revocation of child custody.

Domestic Violence/Aggression,

Marital problems/divorce,

Accidents/injuries,

Financial problems,

Depression/anxiety/chronic anger

Regrettably, a majority of individuals engaged in substance abuse may lack awareness regarding the presence of an underlying anger issue and fail to establish a link between their anger problem and their addiction to alcohol, drugs, and substance abuse.

Hence, they do not actively pursue assistance or obtain support in addressing their anger-related issue. However, frequently their disorder stems from the root cause of their anger.

Anger often precedes the consumption of cocaine and alcohol in many individuals who are dependent on these substances. Anger can be described as a psychological and emotional state of distress that arises when our aspirations and anticipations regarding various aspects of life, individuals, or oneself are obstructed or not realized.

Addictive behavior and substance abuse can be viewed as a coping mechanism employed by individuals to alleviate the distress caused by their anger, wherein they attempt to desensitize themselves through the utilization of drugs, alcohol, and similar substances. This is not a form of anger management; rather, it constitutes self-medication.

When we lack the knowledge of how to effectively control our anger, we attempt to contain the anger within ourselves. Over a period of time, it exacerbates and frequently leads to heightened distressing emotions, including depression and anxiety.

Therefore, the individual has effectively exacerbated their situation by introducing an additional challenge alongside their substance abuse, thus necessitating the implementation of treatment for an additional disorder. There have been numerous scientific investigations that have established the efficacy of anger management interventions in addressing substance abuse issues, leading to a significant decrease in the likelihood of relapse or even complete eradication of such instances.

Medical research has indicated that alcoholism, cocaine addiction, and methamphetamine dependence are medical conditions linked to biochemical alterations in the brain. Conventional treatment methods for substance abuse and alcohol addiction primarily emphasize group therapy and cognitive behavior modification, often overlooking the emotional and physiological factors that contribute to addictive behaviors.

4 – Effective Techniques in Channeling Excess Energy

We have previously conveyed the information to you that anger is widely regarded as a detrimental emotion. We have previously presented various strategies for anger management; however, we have not yet delved into methods for effectively channeling and dissipating anger in a constructive manner. When there is an accumulation of anger within your body, a requisite amount of energy needs to be expended. Certain individuals derive pleasure from engaging in punching a bag, whereas others choose to refrain from partaking in rigorous physical activities. Nevertheless, suppressing anger has far graver consequences than giving oneself permission to acknowledge and release that emotional energy from within.

There exist multiple productive methods through which one can channel their energy. In the subsequent chapter, I will address various approaches that can harness one's anger into generating enthusiasm towards life. It is imperative that you dispose of it. Retaining feelings of anger can induce stress and exert adverse effects on various physiological processes, including digestion, cognitive functioning, and the functioning of the sympathetic nervous system. Are you aware that during the inhalation process, the air typically occupies solely the upper region of the lungs? In the preceding sections on respiratory techniques, we provided guidance for addressing this issue. Nevertheless, there are alternative methods at your disposal to effectively optimize the utilization of the sympathetic nervous system. These approaches facilitate the proper allocation of inhaled oxygen throughout the body, thereby fostering a profound state of physical and mental well-being.

Swimming

In this particular athletic discipline, characterized by its low impact nature, individuals have the opportunity to challenge themselves by setting specific objectives. You may perhaps desire to engage in a swimming activity comprising of two complete laps. You may be inclined to engage in a diving activity from one of the diving platforms available at the swimming pool. May I suggest experimenting with a novel swimming technique? Swimming is advantageous due to its enjoyable nature, as well as its ability to promote proper respiration that stimulates the activation and functionality of the sympathetic nervous system. Additionally, it will be observed that engaging in rigorous physical activity serves to alleviate surplus stress, as well as dissipate nervous energy and anger.

Doing Manual Work

In response to frustration, my father would retreat to the workshop and dedicate his time towards the construction of the boat. Although this might not captivate readers, it is noteworthy that he channeled his restlessness into a constructive endeavor. Likewise, my mother would diligently clean carpets. One can establish personal objectives that involve tasks that are known to be necessary, but often neglected due to lack of time. These objectives can serve as effective outlets for releasing the nervous energy associated with anger. One advantage of this is that it allows for the constructive channeling of this energy, preventing it from festering within oneself and exacerbating its magnitude.

Exercise

Exercise is commonly associated with retribution, but this need not be the case. If one has had the opportunity to witness the television program titled Ally McBeal, one would undoubtedly be acquainted with her peculiar method of managing stress, which involved engaging in a form of rhythmic movement upon her sleeping quarters, donning attire that is unconventional for such a purpose. There is nothing amiss with this. If you desire to engage in an immersive physical activity by playing the most recent YouTube Zumba video and indulging in an uninhibited dance session, then proceed accordingly.

Release the pessimistic energy and demonstrate your liveliness.

Engaging in physical activity while experiencing anger can effectively alleviate that emotional state. Engage in the task of cutting some timber. Engage in the act of planting a few arboreal specimens, diligently tend to the maintenance of the botanical sanctuary, or partake in a leisurely stroll within an undisturbed ecological setting. Cycling also helps. Engaging in these physical activities allows for the restoration of bodily equilibrium and provides an opportunity to detach oneself from anger, enabling a more impartial observation. Once you acquire the ability to accomplish that, you will realize that not only will you derive pleasure from engaging in the physical activity, but it will also contribute to your improved physical well-being and overall happiness. Cease your sedentary habits and your ill-natured disposition. Release that prevailing negativity from your being by physically displacing it through repetitive shaking motions.

Have you ever had the opportunity to experience a water slide? May I inquire about a carnival attraction that elicits fear within you? All of these strategies contribute to the stimulation of adrenaline, which in turn aids in the release of negative energy and facilitates gaining a more objective understanding of things. Think life scares you? Experience the roller coaster ride and allow the refreshing breeze to gracefully caress your hair as you liberate yourself from the burden of detrimental thoughts that fuel aggression. One can relinquish their attachment and, in doing so, discover resolutions that do not cause distress to any individual, but rather effectively address the underlying factors that provoked the initial anger.

It would be beneficial to attain insight into the desires and their consequential impact on the lives of one's peers. The happiness of individuals apart from yourself does not have a direct impact on your own being, nevertheless it is advisable to exhibit logical behavior and express gratitude for the occurrences in one's life.

12. In the event that you experience a sense of exploitation and inadvertently provoke others' anger, it would be wise to empathetically consider their point of view rather than assigning blame. [Aristotle]

In order to gain comprehensive insights into situations and approach them with optimal rationality, we ought to actively engage ourselves in life through the perspectives of others. You are encouraged to attempt to empathize with their perspectives and gain insights into the underlying motivations that drive their behavior.

13. Do not allow yourself to be perturbed if someone conducts themselves in a manner that fails to meet your standards or garner your respect, as doing so may only serve to create distance between you and them. [Horace]

Imposing one's own standards does not guarantee others' respect; rather, individuals will inevitably interact with you based on their own inclinations, irrespective of your efforts to influence such behavior. In order to command respect from others, it is imperative to exhibit kindness and ensure their contentment.

14. Make an effort to perceive events from an alternate perspective, and refrain from becoming annoyed by meaningless, unfunny jokes. [Sidonius]

In order to interact with others in a rational manner, it is advisable to find amusement in situations where they may seem absurd. In the event someone levies a jesting insult toward you, it is advisable to expeditiously overcome any adverse impact it may have.

15. When engaging with individuals who are angered, it is advised to refrain from internalizing their sentiments and

endeavor to empathize with their point of view. [Seneca]

In order to engage in rational interactions with others, it is crucial to employ all possible means to prevent them from inducing feelings of guilt within you for actions you did not commit. It is imperative that you direct your attention towards the core elements and acknowledge the endeavors of others.

16. Frequently, individuals who harbor anger towards you are experiencing emotional distress, and they are merely employing a means of self-expression as a way to alleviate their suffering. [Epicurus]

Whilst acknowledging its challenging nature, it is important to recognize that the majority of individuals exhibiting anger towards you typically possess valid justifications for their sentiments. It is advisable to endeavor to comprehend the underlying reasons behind their behavior and then assess whether you wish to disregard them or make efforts to restore their happiness.

17. In the event that an individual causes distress in your life, endeavor to consider the situation from their standpoint and refrain from internalizing it as a personal offense. [Seneca]

One must consistently endeavor to perceive things from the viewpoint of others and comprehend the underlying motivations that influence their behavior towards oneself. They might perceive the need to cause you distress, or they might engage in behaviors that are deemed acceptable by those in their social circle.

18. Do not succumb to fear in the face of others' anger, and remain steadfast in upholding your values despite any attempts to undermine them. [Epicurus]

In order to uphold your principles, it is imperative not to be intimidated by the ire of others, but rather to endeavor to empathize with their viewpoint. It is imperative to adopt measures to prevent the imposition of unwarranted guilt onto oneself by others for actions not committed, while consistently upholding principled standards.

For the purpose of relinquishing internal impediments that hinder the process of recovery, it is imperative that you possess the willingness to introspect and discern the precise nature of your ailment. On occasion, the diligent practice of introspection yields unexpected outcomes. For instance, do you genuinely harbor anger towards your spouse for their tardiness to dinner, or are you experiencing anger due to the implications of these actions, which have left you feeling insignificant, unnoticed, and disregarded? It is crucial to establish these distinctions. It is imperative to have a clear understanding of the precise reasons underlying your anger, as well as the individuals towards whom this anger is directed.

In my collegiate experience, there was a particular professor who appeared to harbor aversion towards me without any discernible cause. The professor's evident bias against me appeared to border on emotional impairment. However, following a meeting with that professor, I discovered that I evoked a sense of familiarity in this person, reminiscent of a cherished spouse who had passed away just a short time ago. The professor administered disciplinary measures towards me, as the mere sight of me evoked distressing emotions within their heart.

Occasionally, individuals may harbor anger towards you for matters that are entirely beyond your control. I was unable to control my appearance, nor could I control the fact that when the professor glanced at me, they perceived a depiction of their beloved gradually deteriorating and succumbing to a dreadful cancer. However, upon discovering the reason behind my professor's anger, I found it effortless to sympathize with the circumstances. Moreover, subsequent to engaging in dialogue with me, the professor came to the realization that there was a distinct sense of rekindling the positive attributes of their late spouse when interacting with me. The professor's initial displays of anger gradually transformed into a profuse shedding of tears, during which they expressed their desire for us to maintain contact, in order to sustain what they perceived as an enduring connection with a cherished portion of their academic community. Upon resolution of this anger, an invaluable opportunity for healing and personal development was afforded to the parties involved.

Releasing can prove to be quite challenging. Occasionally, life imposes excessive expectations upon us. We are tasked with parting ways from cherished family and friends—we are tasked with parting ways from occupations, residences, aspirations... at times, soldiers are even tasked with surrendering body extremities, and fundamental emotional facets of their being. Frequently, the expression of anger is deemed as justified.

The peril arises when the sentiment of anger is translated into concrete actions. For example, in the event that I am able to tactfully embrace and endure my emotions of anger, allowing the sensation to pass through me until the sentiment dissipates, it is highly unlikely that any substantial or enduring damage will be inflicted. Nevertheless, should my anger serve as a catalyst for me to wield a knife and engage in an act of tire-slashing within a parking lot, a multitude of undesirable repercussions may ensue. It is possible that I could be apprehended and incarcerated. There exists a possibility that I will be compelled to bear the financial burden for the entire set of tires that I vandalized, thereby potentially plunging myself into a state of indebtedness, and so forth. It becomes significantly more convenient to allow the sentiment to permeate my being, until it ultimately dissipates on its own accord.

Consider, for example, the situation of an individual who served in the United States Marine Corps, with whom I had the opportunity to acquaintance in the past. This individual returned from the conflict in Iraq with numerous challenges. Having witnessed explosions occurring in close proximity and experiencing the tragic loss of a companion due to an act of terrorism, this individual returned with a considerable amount of resentment residing within their being. He appeared to be discontented with the U.S's intervention in this situation, harboring dissatisfaction due to unmet expectations arising from his enlistment. He had anticipated that his tenure in the military would ensure his financial stability, yet instead he returned to find himself burdened by an overwhelming accumulation of debt. Moreover, in addition to everything else, he had incurred the unfortunate loss of a limb during combat, thereby experiencing a profound sense of identity deprivation as an individual engaged in athletics and physical fitness pursuits.

Effectively Managing Anger Through The Acquisition Of The Ability To Experience Annoyance.

The most gentle manifestation of anger is irritation. It constitutes a complete antithesis to rage and offers improved means for the management of annoyance.

The majority of individuals experience a greater sense of frustration rather than anger. It exhibits a relatively subdued emotional state, distinct from anger, wherein individuals often overcome this sentiment without taking proactive measures to address it.

Experiencing frustration does not pose an issue as long as it remains at that stage. The effective management of anger can be achieved through its transformation into annoyance. Allow me to explain the process to achieve this:

• Avoid placing excessive significance on the situation or incident. It is imperative to prevent oneself from being easily affected or perturbed by external stimuli. In the event of accidental contact by another individual that results in the displacement of your belongings, it may cause a level of frustration, but it is possible to alleviate this inconvenience.

• Please refrain from associating this matter with your personal identity. • Avoid drawing conclusions that attribute this matter to your individual character.
• Please understand that this issue

should not be interpreted as a reflection of your personal qualities or characteristics. • It is important to dissociate this matter from your personal identity. The individual who unintentionally collided with you did not do so out of animosity or dislike towards you. It does not pertain to your personal character.

• Refrain from attributing fault to others. • Avoid assigning responsibility to others. • Abstain from holding others accountable. • Desist from placing the blame on others. When one discovers the inclination to assign blame to others, it is advisable to halt such a tendency and relinquish it.

• Refrain from engaging in schemes of retribution. The typical consequence of the act of blaming others is devising plans for retaliation. Seeking retribution is not a worthwhile endeavor, considering the amount of energy invested in it.

- Acquire the ability to maintain composure in challenging circumstances and avoid succumbing to anger. You find it vexing that the individual you encountered accidentally collided with you. It has the potential to rapidly escalate into a state of anger if one lacks the ability to effectively direct their attention towards diffusing the circumstances. Contemplating a visit to the nearest coffee establishment to partake in your preferred beverage may serve as a distraction from the aforementioned incident.

- Cease harboring self-pity. • Refrain from indulging in self-pity. • Discontinue the self-pitying behavior. • Abstain from wallowing in self-pity. • Desist from entertaining self-pity. Considering oneself as the wronged party would incite feelings of anger. Redirect your focus towards another subject matter, thus ensuring the prevention of harboring any feelings of anger.

- Avoid allowing your prevailing negative emotions to overpower the current circumstance. Do not succumb to anger solely based on feelings of melancholy. Remind yourself that the situation should solely be viewed as an irksome inconvenience and nothing more.

Mastering the art of transforming anger into annoyance may prove to be a process that demands a significant investment of time. Nonetheless, one's unwavering commitment and self-control will ultimately yield the invaluable outcome of this advantageous alteration. If you possess a propensity for quicker agitation, it becomes imperative for you to exhibit heightened diligence in order to sustain this state of being irritated rather than enraged. You are permitted to express your irritation by stamping your feet, but that comprises the extent of your allowed behavior.

Value 6 – The Value of Mitigating Violence: Anger can be utilized as a means to prevent or ameliorate acts of violence. Anger functions as a mode of social communication, frequently indicating the presence of unresolved matters that require attention. The display of anger in an individual serves as a signal that there is an underlying problem, thereby facilitating those who are emotionally resilient to potentially address the matter before it intensifies.

Value 7 - Consciousness Value: Anger serves to heighten our awareness of the wrongs or injustices that have been perpetrated against us. When our rights are denied by others, we experience feelings of insult, disrespect, or exploitation, which often leads to a sense of anger. Rage serves as an introspective compass, shedding light upon the injustices inflicted upon us by others, thereby highlighting the imperative to address and resolve such matters. Upon recognizing the injustice that has been inflicted upon us, we promptly notify the individuals implicated, thus mitigating the potential recurrence of such occurrences in the future. By means of this consciousness, we can proactively mitigate instances of exploitation and deceit. We elicit the finest contributions from individuals by cultivating an atmosphere wherein they are unable to exploit our vulnerability, as we possess astute awareness of their misguided actions. The promotion of consciousness can facilitate a societal transformation and result in an escalation of the societal repercussions of misconduct.

Value 8 – Preservation of Values and Beliefs: As previously discussed, anger serves as both an indicator and regulator of social and personal values. Additionally, wrath serves as a safeguard for our principles. When we are confronted with specific circumstances that are incongruent with our belief and value framework, the emotion of anger serves as a catalyst, prompting us to undertake corrective measures in order to rectify the situation.

Value 9 – Enhancement of Interpersonal Bonds: Just as the detrimental effects of anger can potentially lead to the dissolution of a relationship, it is equally possible for anger to serve as a catalyst for strengthening and fortifying the bond between individuals. To obtain this outcome of value through anger, the key lies in channeling your anger constructively. When anger is appropriately employed, it often enables the resolution of misunderstandings, prompting the individuals involved to attentively heed and align with your viewpoint. When the assertive manner is employed, anger serves to cultivate a connection within a relationship. It is a form that pertains to a mutually beneficial outcome. By striving for mutual advantages, you will consequently garner their esteem.

Value 10 - Value of Self-awareness: Anger can offer us valuable insights into our fundamental challenges. Anger typically arises from an underlying cause, which often translates into the furious demeanor we exhibit. Anger provides us with the capacity to introspect and discern the underlying core obstacle. By ascertaining the origins of emotions such as fear, offense, or frustration, one can facilitate their resolution and achieve a state of contentment in life. Furthermore, the intrinsic worth of such insight is exemplified by the fact that anger fosters personal growth and development. It is more convenient to address these areas of improvement and further develop our personal growth, having acknowledged our weaknesses and obstacles.

9 - DOCUMENT YOUR IRE

Anger is inevitable. Research findings have indicated that the manifestation of anger can negatively impact one's overall well-being. A study conducted by scholars from Yale University has demonstrated that individuals who struggle with anger management are prone to experiencing higher rates of illness due to a compromised immune system. It is imperative that you partake in a physical activity, as indicated in the preceding section, to appropriately release any pent-up feelings of anger. In addition to physical activity, it is advisable to cultivate the practice of documenting one's feelings of anger in a journal at the close of each day.

Although it may appear futile to document your anger, this approach can prove to be highly effective when executed properly. It is important to bear in mind that our purpose in writing this letter is not to incite animosity or seek retribution by documenting the actions of those who wronged you.

Engaging in the act of articulating your feelings of anger through writing would assist in enhancing your ability to effectively convey your emotions on paper. It will assist you in discerning the individuals, subjects, or stimuli that typically elicit your feelings of anger. Another crucial benefit of documenting one's anger is that it alleviates mental burdens by preventing continual rumination. Taking the time to jot down your thoughts will facilitate a more structured approach to the issue, permitting you to direct your attention towards other pressing matters.

Nevertheless, it is imperative to meticulously record the entire sequence of events from the very beginning when documenting your anger in a journal. This will aid in enhancing your analytical abilities. If it is your practice to keep a daily journal, it is advised that you also maintain a separate journal specifically dedicated to recording instances of anger. By keeping a separate journal, you can effectively direct your attention towards the challenges encountered.

You have the option to either keep a physical hard cover journal or utilize a digital counterpart. In my personal preference, I find that utilizing a hardcover journal facilitates a stronger sense of self-connection.

When documenting it in a journal, please make sure to incorporate the following guidelines:

Who made me angry

What was the subject matter that instigated it?

Where was I

What was the statement made by the individual?

How I feel

How did I react

The aforementioned pointers lack a conclusive nature. Feel at liberty to include as many additional points as you desire. This will assist you in enhancing your ability to analyze your actions. Merely transcribing information into your journal is insufficient. It is imperative that we engage in regular reviews of the journal to monitor prevalent concerns. Once recognized, you can deliberately determine the appropriate course of action when confronted with comparable, if not identical, circumstances.

As an illustration, an individual might categorize you as mendacious or devoid of shame. If such comments are consistently appearing in your journal, it is imperative to investigate the underlying causes that have led individuals to make these statements. Consequently, this will assist you in formulating viable courses of action. It is also possible for you to deduce that an individual is intentionally engaging in such activities with the motive of defaming your reputation. This will provide you with additional insight into whether it is advisable for you to maintain a distance from such an individual.

In conclusion, it is crucial to emphasize the significance of expressing anger through journaling in an appropriate and descriptive manner. This can assist you in implementing a systematic approach to effectively managing the factors that trigger your anger.

1. Acquire familiarity with your anger indicators: By familiarizing yourself with your anger indicators, you can readily discern when you are on the verge of experiencing an episode of anger or outburst. The fundamental indicators consist of heightened heartbeat, elevated heart rate, and in certain individuals, the onset of tingling sensations in their palms. When you discern any of these indicators, it indicates that your anger is intensifying and you may be on the

verge of experiencing an outburst. Being aware of its imminent arrival enables you to anticipate and preempt its occurrence, thereby thwarting any unforeseen impacts.

2. Allow some time to elapse before responding: This bears similarity to imposing a temporary respite on oneself, signifying the need to cultivate the ability to restrain immediate impulses towards anger in response to a given situation. When experiencing an escalation of your anger, endeavor to restrain it and engage in a deliberate process of numerically counting from one to ten prior to responding. Engaging in a sequential numerical count from 1 to 10 facilitates the rapid dissipation of one's escalating anger.

3. Engage in deep and deliberate inhalation: As one approaches the verge of an outburst fueled by anger,

respiration tends to deviate from its natural rhythm, becoming increasingly unpredictable and irregular. Therefore, it is imperative that you acquire the ability to regulate your breathing prior to proceeding with any course of action. By consciously regulating your breath, you can effectively mitigate the activation of anger signals, cultivate a state of tranquility, and, crucially, sustain an unwavering adherence to rational thinking, thereby promoting clear and reasoned decision-making.

4. Muscle Relaxation. When experiencing anger, exert deliberate effort to achieve muscular relaxation. The initial measure to accomplish this objective involves loosening your grip. The act of involuntarily clenching one's fist in moments of anger appears to be an instinctive response that subconsciously readies an individual for combat. Loosening your muscles conveys signals

to your brain that you are in a state of relaxation and in control of the situation. This simple action is likely to result in more rational behavior rather than emotional reaction. In the most straightforward manner, you would have managed to subdue a wild and fervent emotion.

Fundamental Factors That May Contribute To Challenges In Anger Management

Individuals employ varied strategies to manage daily challenges, encompassing both emotionally and physically taxing situations they have encountered. Certain individuals may choose to retreat and isolate themselves from their external environment, either through physical removal or mental disengagement. Externally, they may exude an air of sourness, irritability, cruelty, and an apparent inclination towards hot-headedness.

Psychological concerns perpetuate in a cyclical manner, often originating from seemingly inconsequential adversities. It is possible that we believe we have addressed the issue, yet remain unaware of the lasting impact it has had on our mental well-being. With every encounter we undergo, we undergo a gradual transformation, gaining valuable insights and striving to mature as we navigate through it. It is, ultimately, the means through which we experience personal growth and cultivate our character over the course of our lives. It is worth noting that even the slightest scar can effectively conceal a delicate or potentially infectious wound. Every negative encounter will gradually compound the issue, leading to a severe contamination that manifests in diverse emotional expressions. These emotional concerns might be the underlying factors contributing to an individual's challenges with anger management.

Anxiety

Anxiety can serve as a fundamental emotional concern that contributes to anger, just as anger can be a catalyst for anxiety. Individuals afflicted with anxiety exhibit tendencies towards excessive worrying and engage in anticipatory apprehension long before the actual occurrence of events. They often exhibit a propensity to become preoccupied with a specific issue, leading them to experience excessive anxiety regarding potential future outcomes or ongoing situations. Additionally, individuals often exhibit a tendency to become preoccupied with future outcomes, thereby losing sight of the present moment. Consequently, they may encounter challenges when attempting to maintain focus and concentration.

Low Self-Esteem

Individuals who experience low self-esteem often harbor a perception that the entire world would be more prosperous without their presence. Lacking in self-assurance and self-esteem, individuals may display sensitivity, perceiving even minor incidents as personal offenses. In addition, they may demonstrate passive-aggressive tendencies through the utilization of insults and sarcasm as a means of dealing with their perceived shortcomings or instances when they perceive themselves as victimized.

Trust Issues

Individuals who possess a lack of trust tend to encounter challenges when forming intimate connections, exhibiting behaviors such as jealousy, suspicion, and a persistent propensity to interrogate others in pursuit of validating their actions and seeking the truth. Their lack of trust in individuals results in fractured or highly tumultuous interpersonal connections, owing to their proclivity for harsh scrutiny.

History of Abuse

Individuals who have experienced abuse often exhibit elevated levels of anger, lack of trust, and may demonstrate behaviours that are detrimental in nature. They may encounter difficulties pertaining to intimacy, interpersonal connections, challenges related to self-worth, as well as issues concerning the management of anger.

History of Violence

Individuals with a documented record of violent behavior may potentially be affected by an underlying issue of considerable complexity, which encompasses emotional, mental, or physical aspects. Typically, individuals tend to react strongly when they perceive a threat or experience a sense of insecurity.

One - Exploring the Concept of Anger

Every human being is capable of feeling various emotions - from happiness to sadness, from love to hate and from excitement to fear.

However, what distinguishes your emotional experience from that of others is the manner in which you articulate and convey your emotions.

One has the choice to experience personal happiness and keep it internalized, or embrace joy and partake in communal celebrations. The process of anger manifestation is akin in nature.

Anger is a potent sentiment that arises as a reaction to an adverse circumstance. This response may arise as a result of encountering a challenging or demanding situation, harboring apprehensions, experiencing distressing cognitive patterns, or being burdened by feelings of anxiety, which may be specifically directed at a particular individual or object.

Anger is widely perceived as an adverse emotion owing to its association with instances of individuals engaging in aggressive behaviors during such states.

They vocalize vehemently towards unsuspecting individuals, cause harm to their cherished ones, and engage in the act of annihilating any object they come into contact with.

What is the cause behind people experiencing anger? There are numerous provocations of anger, and as you engage with this text, you may have already recollected certain instances that have incited anger within you.

The demanding nature of your job, the increasing expenses you face, and the unwavering behavior of your dog can all contribute to your heightened emotional state. Similar to other emotional states, anger is underpinned by a physiological foundation.

It is facilitated by specific chemicals that are secreted by the brain in response to a stimulus as part of an individual's sympathetic reaction.

These chemical substances encompass epinephrine and norepinephrine, which are referred to as adrenaline and noradrenaline correspondingly.

They are accountable for the escalation of your heart rate and the heightening of your blood pressure during instances of anger.

Due to the heightened intensity of this emotional state, anger becomes arduous to regulate.

Episodes of abrupt anger can result in a disregard for societal conventions and legal principles, potentially fostering tendencies towards aggression. Nevertheless, it is incumbent upon men to exercise authority over their emotions, particularly when it comes to managing their anger.

There are diverse methods through which one can articulate their anger without resorting to adverse reactions. Acquiring the skills to effectively regulate and address anger in its entirety may require a substantial investment of time and dedication. However, the long-term benefits it holds are undeniably capable of greatly enhancing your overall life experience.

Please proceed to the subsequent page to acquire knowledge regarding the five sequential measures on effectively managing and regulating one's anger.

Constructive Problem Resolution

Individuals who perceive life's adversities as opportunities for growth and personal development have embraced a constructive approach in resolving societal issues. These individuals typically exhibit a disposition characterized by optimism, patience, as well as a strong determination to achieve their desired outcomes. They possess a considerate and deliberate demeanor towards life, and their decisions are not swayed by sentiments of anger.

Bernie, a senior citizen in his late sixties who had worked as a car salesperson and was now retired, exuded an air of joviality, sociability, and intellectual acuity. However, he had encountered numerous challenges and adversities throughout the course of his lifetime. At the age of twenty-four, he entered into matrimony with his long-term romantic partner from high school, thereby culminating in a state of utmost blissfulness for the couple. However, during Bernie's early thirties, he experienced the sudden and unforeseen loss of his spouse, which consequently placed the responsibility of raising their three children solely on his shoulders.

Bernie entered into a new marital union within a span of three years, this time with a lady hailing from the automotive dealership where he held employment.

The dissolution of his second marriage occurred prior to the birth of another child. Throughout his years of employment, Bernie dedicated a significant portion of his earnings towards the financial support and upbringing of his children. Additionally, he experienced the typical fluctuations and challenges associated with raising children, overseeing a household, and progressing in his professional journey. In his fifties, Bernie had acquired a discernible composure when faced with adversity. When confronted with a challenge, he successfully tapped into his innate sense of wonder, allowing him to identify the optimal solution that would yield the most favorable outcomes. Primarily, he opted to abstain from immediate or emotive responses to issues. Alternatively, he would opt for a strategic approach, temporarily withdrawing himself from the situation. This method frequently enabled him to redirect his efforts towards conducting thorough research at reputable libraries or online platforms, as well as seeking guidance from reliable acquaintances on the best course of action tailored to the specific circumstances.

Bernie consistently exhibited a commitment to continuous learning and personal development. Each of his challenges presented a fresh opportunity for the acquisition and refinement of his skills and knowledge. He consistently demonstrated resourcefulness in addressing obstacles and seldom exacerbated complex circumstances. Each of Bernie's four children successfully completed their high school education with commendable academic performance, and subsequently enrolled in nearby institutions of higher learning. Currently, there is an individual who has embraced the profession of an accountant, another who has chosen the vocation of a teacher, a third who has taken on the responsibilities of a stay-at-home mother, and the youngest sibling has pursued a career in the automobile industry, much akin to Bernie's chosen path. Over time, due to his problem-solving methodology, Bernie established himself as a prominent figure whom others frequently approached for counsel.

The Six Phases of Social Problem Resolution

In relation to the analysis of an anger episode, it is important to consider six key components, namely a trigger event, cognitive processes, subjective experience, an impulse to take action, the expression of anger, and the resulting outcomes. The social problem-solving process entails six procedural steps:

Thoroughly ascertain the issue

Ascertain potential remedies

Determine probable immediate consequences of the proposed resolutions.

Determine the probable long-term ramifications of your prospective resolutions.

Choose the optimal resolution and implement it effectively.

The solution provided requires a thorough appraisal.

Thoroughly ascertain the issue at hand.

When one acknowledges a persistent societal issue, what is being essentially done is recognizing a source of personal emotional agitation. In order to precisely, definitively, and impartially ascertain a trigger, one may employ the when-then structure. This entails describing the specific circumstance using the "when" component, and proceeding with an account of one's subsequent response. By employing this structure, one can initiate their concentration on the problem at hand and subsequently develop a comprehension of one's personal responses. Additionally, it affords you the opportunity to recount the events without superfluous embellishments, such as assigning culpability or magnifying the significance of the situation.

When employing the when-then structure, it is crucial to singularly identify one issue at any given time. As a result, it is necessary for you to restart the initial part of step 1 for each problem that you identify. Formulating a problem in the when-then format may pose challenges on occasion, yet with careful consideration, one can invariably accomplish this task.

As an illustration, consider the scenario in which you encounter persistent and unwanted communication from your former spouse, who repeatedly initiates contact with the intention to harass you and engage in disputes. You may ascertain the issue by asserting, 'I desire cessation of all contact initiated by my former spouse,' yet this declaration lacks the necessary level of specificity for effective problem-solving. However, the problem can be reframed as follows: "Upon receiving derogatory remarks during phone conversations with my former spouse, arguments ensue, causing me to experience anger, a sense of perpetuated misery, and a lingering feeling of dissatisfaction throughout the remainder of the day."

Progressing through Successive Stages

Previously, our attention was directed towards Piaget's developmental stages. Although informative, we have also reached the conclusion that these stages do not comprehensively encompass the entirety of a child's narrative. Fortunate tidings are bestowed upon us as contemporary psychology has bestowed upon us a significantly enhanced comprehension of the various stages of a child's development.

Contemporary researchers commonly classify the stages of children's development into five principal categories. Kindly be advised that there are no difference observed between these groups and Piaget's work. If anything, these stages serve to enhance and expand upon the profundity of Piaget's original contributions.

Consequently, based on the insights of contemporary scholars, let us proceed to thoroughly examine the five phases encompassing child development.

1. Newborn

The infancy period is an exceptionally thrilling phase for both offspring and their caretakers. During this phase, young individuals actively explore and familiarize themselves with their surroundings. Parents also discover the remarkable transformation their child is swiftly undergoing. Infants, in their initial month of life, exhibit responses to the external stimuli in their environment. They respond to auditory, visual, and tactile stimuli. At this juncture, it is imperative to establish contact as a means of communication with children. Given that young children do not possess developed language skills, it becomes imperative to utilize alternative modes of communication, such as physical contact in the form of gentle touching, embracing, cuddling, and displaying affection through gestures like kissing, as a means to express their feelings.

The sensory perception of young individuals undergoes rapid development during this particular phase. During the initial half-year period, there is observable enhancement in their visual acuity as well as olfactory capabilities. Furthermore, as infants explore the capabilities of their limbs, neck, and hands, they begin to demonstrate the development of motor skills. Parents may also identify developmental disabilities during this initial phase. Therefore, it is imperative to closely monitor restricted physical mobility or absence thereof.

On an emotional level, children express their feelings through tears and smiles. Typically, shedding tears is the primary mode of communication employed to convey distress. Children also express their desires or needs by means of tears. Additionally, it is worth noting that children express their pleasure by means of smiling and laughing. An illustration of this can be observed in the behavior of infants, where they exhibit a smile as an expression of recognition for their parents, siblings, grandparents, or objects that capture their fondness and interest.

The initial phase of infancy span approximately three months. The initial phase is an exceptional period. However, it is equally essential/significant/vital. It is imperative that parents make diligent efforts to engage their children through auditory, visual, and tactile experiences. By carrying out this action, it aids in the enhancement of children's cognitive and physical abilities, ultimately facilitating their transition into early childhood.

Allow me to impart the valuable insights I have gained through my extensive tenure as a parent.

First and foremost, it is important for newborns to distinguish and recognize the individuals in their immediate environment. It is, consequently, imperative for parents to engage in dialogue with their newborn infants.

Infants possess the ability to readily discern their mothers' voices. Ultimately, their mothers' voices were the only ones they heard for a duration of nine months. It is imperative for fathers to allocate time for engaging in conversations with their newborn infants. Specifically, expressions such as "I am your mother" or "I am your father" significantly contribute to the newborns' ability to recognize their environment. The act of presenting infants with items and identifying them by their respective names enables them to adapt to their surroundings.

At this juncture, I urge you to engage in the act of reading stories to your child. Please do not hesitate to present them with illustrated depictions from storybooks while engaging in reading sessions. Your infant may not possess complete cognitive comprehension of the narrative's substance. However, by consistently exposing your baby to language, you can significantly enhance their linguistic abilities.

2. Infancy

Significant developments occur during the initial stages of infancy. The stage of infancy generally spans from three months to a year. In this particular phase, infants undergo a process of gradually reducing their reliance on their primary caregiver and developing a certain degree of independence.

In the early stages of their development, infants commence the process of discerning and mastering movement. They possess the ability to consciously regulate the movements of their upper and lower extremities. Furthermore, there is a significant increase in both head and neck movements. By the time they reach the age of six months, the majority of infants are capable of sitting up on their own without support and might begin demonstrating indications of mobility through crawling.

Security is a fundamental aspect in the early stages of life. Moreover, prioritizing the safety of your child, such as by ensuring the removal of any sharp objects within their reach, is crucial. Concurrently, it is equally essential to grant children the autonomy they require as they embark on their journey of mobility. They require the presence of their caregiver in close proximity, yet without causing any interruption. It affords children the opportunity to navigate their surroundings without constraints, simultaneously assuring them of a vigilant presence for their protection. This methodology proves to be highly efficacious in fostering a child's autonomy.

During the infancy stage, it is noteworthy to mention that babies possess an inherent inclination towards exploring their surroundings by reaching out and grasping objects within their vicinity. Children of this age possess a receptive inclination to embrace anything that captivates their interest. Consequently, it would not be unexpected for your child to abruptly seize your spectacles from your countenance.

Indicators of developmental challenges may encompass restricted range of motion or delayed reactivity. However, it should be noted that children develop and mature at varying rates. So, it is imperative to closely monitor the child's developmental advancements throughout this phase.

Volatile anger

This is the kind of anger that seems to emanate out of specific nothingness. Frequently, individuals become angered by matters of both substantial and trivial nature. Once this form of violence is impulsive in nature, it also dissipates rapidly.

Regrettably, this particular form of anger can exude detrimental consequences. This is because individuals in your vicinity will recognize the necessity of maintaining distance from you due to apprehension about provoking your anger. If left unattended, it has the potential to trigger hazardous detonations.

To address this resentment, it is necessary to meticulously ascertain the indicators and manifestations that precede these displays of rage. Subsequently, determine how you can proficiently employ relaxation strategies to manage and mitigate the escalating and ultimately eruptive anger.

Indignation as an alternative emotional response

Were you aware that anger can occasionally serve as a substitute emotion? You may be pondering, "However, what do you intend to convey through the phrase 'substitute emotion'?" At times, individuals frequently experience anger as a means to evade confronting their emotional distress. In lieu of permitting oneself to harbor regret over one's suffering, one elects to substitute said suffering with anger, given that the experience of anger is relatively more endurable than that of pain. It may occur in a deliberate or inadvertent manner.

Anger can serve as a beneficial coping mechanism due to its ability to distract individuals from experiencing pain, resulting in several advantages. When one is experiencing discomfort, their thoughts are consumed by the sensation of their discomfort. Nevertheless, if one experiences anger, it becomes effortless to contemplate causing harm to those individuals who have inflicted pain upon them. To put it differently, there is a discernible change in the allocation of attention, transitioning from self-orientation to directing it towards others.

Hence, it is imperative to acknowledge that anger merely provides a transient shield for individuals to evade the recognition, resolution, and management of their genuine distressing emotions. You exclusively prioritize seeking vengeance. Nevertheless, it is crucial to bear in mind that expressing anger serves as a pivotal mechanism for concealing the daunting reality and inherent vulnerability elicited by the current circumstances.

Moreover, to the extent that anger serves as a capable disguise for vulnerability, it also engenders specific sentiments of moral superiority, righteousness, and potency, characteristics that are lacking when an individual experiences suffering. In essence, when experiencing anger, there is justification for feeling such anger. To put it differently, during periods of anger, your prevailing thoughts revolve around the notion that individuals who have inflicted harm upon you ought to face appropriate consequences. It is a challenging task to encounter individuals who harbor anger towards others who have not inflicted considerable damage upon them.

What are the advantages and disadvantages of anger?

With regards to anger, given its inherent negative nature, it is accompanied by several advantages, encompassing aspects such as social interactions, well-being, and emotional status. Regardless of the legitimacy of your passion, it is the alluring sensation of righteousness that enhances our self-esteem and alleviates our ego.

In reality, experiencing anger often provides a sense of gratification, as it allows one to avoid confronting the distressing sensation of vulnerability. One can exclusively harness their anger to transform states of vulnerability and helplessness into authority and mastery. Certain individuals may cultivate an inherent tendency to instigate feelings of anger in susceptible individuals as a means of evading genuine challenges.

Nevertheless, the issue lies in the fact that despite anger serving as a diversion from the truth (vulnerability), one continues to experience and perceive vulnerability to a certain degree. To clarify, transforming your pain into anger does not guarantee the immediate alleviation of your pain. It diverts your attention momentarily from that. Please bear in mind that expressing anger is not a constructive solution to address the root cause of your fear and vulnerability. It gives rise to a novel challenge that has the potential to impact your social, emotional, and physical welfare.

Yielding in order to prevent emotional upheaval rather than out of genuine affection and concern for the individual.

Unfortunately, individuals who struggle with anger management might discover that they receive concessions or compliance from others as a result of others' desire to avoid confronting or managing the outbursts and emotional volatility. This becomes more apparent when interacting with individuals beyond the confines of your personal connections, such as those outside your immediate circle such as relatives and close acquaintances. It is conceivable that there may be others who perceive the manifestation of anger in your partner, or potentially even within yourself, judging by the responses elicited from individuals in relation to your behavior and emotional expressions. This is a matter of which you should also be cognizant.

The incapacity to derive pleasure from customary pursuits.

Additional contributors to feelings of anger include stress and tension. When an individual becomes upset or enraged, their emotions permeate even the most basic tasks, burdening them with an aura of anger and greatly diminishing the quality of their life, although it should not be the case.

Hence, inaction prevails and if not, any endeavor towards its accomplishment resembles a maritime anchor that hinders the ship's journey towards the shore. This could potentially result in a disagreement as well.

Serious aggression issues.

Failure to manage your anger appropriately may lead to the manifestation of aggression, which can manifest itself through acts of physical or emotional abuse. It is by no means a straightforward affair. This can manifest as derogatory labeling, harassment, coercive tactics, issuing threats, hurling objects, causing physical damage, or inflicting harm upon another individual, to put it plainly.

An additional facet to consider pertains to passive-aggressive conduct, exemplified by employing the "silent treatment," forcefully shutting doors to manifest anger, and engaging in self-centered actions with the intention of garnering sympathy.

The veracity regarding this situation can be summarized as follows: in the absence of curbing anger and implementing a resolution, the consequences can escalate into grave circumstances, including matters of life and death. It is undesirable for the situation to escalate to this extent; therefore, if you observe the initial signs of such undesirable conduct, it is plausible that the individual is seeking assistance, and it is important to offer support. In the event that you are unable to render assistance, facilitate their search for a suitable individual who can aid them in the most effective manner. Each and every individual is entitled to experience a state of tranquility and increased moments of happiness.

Children Diagnosed With Attention Deficit Hyperactivity Disorder (Adhd) And Exhibiting Challenges In Regulating Their Anger.

Indeed, even an infant has the capacity to express distress by means of vocalization when awakening with hunger and not receiving immediate nourishment. As per the shared understanding amongst fatigued caregivers of infants, babies vocalize their discomfort due to a variety of reasons such as hunger, the desire for physical contact, or the need for a diaper change. Additionally, cries may also signify fatigue, illness, or physical discomfort. Furthermore, certain infants exhibit a heightened aversive response to their external environment. Consequently, the infant displays signs of irritability and dependency. Typically, genuine displays of temper only manifest when an infant reaches the age of 12 to 18 months. The irate wailing of your infant may resemble a miniature version of an adult. If your infant displays restlessness and irritability throughout the day, without the need for feeding or a diaper change, it is possible that they require a means of releasing excess energy. Certain infants cry as a means to alleviate stress or expend surplus energy, while others merely require crying in order to induce slumber.

Nevertheless, the occurrence of temper tantrums in toddlers cannot always be attributed solely to the aforementioned factors; it could also potentially stem from a mental disorder. Indeed, it is commonly referred to as ADHD, which stands for attention deficit hyperactivity disorder. It is not unusual for children diagnosed with ADHD to experience bouts of intense anger. Determining this can be challenging at times, as toddlers often encounter difficulties in sustaining their attention. Typically, toddlers are not commonly diagnosed with attention deficit hyperactivity disorder (ADHD). Nevertheless, certain behaviors exhibited by toddlers may give rise to parental concerns regarding the presence of ADHD or the potential for its development.

Nevertheless, ADHD encompasses more than the customary conduct exhibited by young children. Per the findings of the National Institutes of Health (NIH), adolescents and even individuals of mature age can experience the aforementioned condition. It is of utmost importance to recognize the signs of ADHD in early childhood. These youngsters might encounter difficulty in effectively managing and controlling their emotions. They may exhibit heightened sensitivity as well. Challenging or exasperating circumstances can swiftly result in outbursts of frustration. Children diagnosed with attention deficit hyperactivity disorder (ADHD) also encounter challenges in exercising self-control and engaging in reflective problem-solving prior to responding. As per the National Institutes of Health (NIH), the subsequent are the three predominant indicators of the ailment amongst children aged three and above:

Inattention.

Hyperactivity.

Impulsivity.

These behaviors are also observed in children who are not diagnosed with ADHD. The condition will not be diagnosed in your child unless the symptoms persist for a duration exceeding six months and significantly hinder their ability to engage in activities that are appropriate for their age. When conducting a diagnosis of attention deficit hyperactivity disorder (ADHD) in a child below the age of five, it is imperative to exercise great care, particularly when contemplating the use of medication. It is advisable that a child psychiatrist or a specialized pediatrician with expertise in behavior and development be consulted for an accurate diagnosis at this early stage. Please note, however, that certain child psychiatrists may refrain from making a diagnosis until the child has commenced their education, as one crucial aspect of diagnosing ADHD is the presence of symptoms across multiple environments. An instance of this can be seen when the child displays symptoms both in domestic and educational settings, or in the presence of a caregiver as well as acquaintances or kinfolk.

▷ Benefits of employing an authoritative parenting style

According to a research investigation, it has been indicated that children who receive upbringing from authoritative parents exhibit higher levels of self-confidence and self-esteem. This phenomenon can be attributed to the notion that parents with an authoritative parenting style establish an environment that facilitates the open expression of their children's opinions and perspectives in regards to decisions pertaining to them. Children residing in these households experience a sense of safety and emotional stability.

Furthermore, multiple research studies have demonstrated that children residing in such households exhibit a notable degree of emotional intelligence. An essential characteristic observed in these parents is their inclination to assist children in overcoming obstacles rather than entirely eliminate the obstacles on their behalf. Over a period of time, children acquire enhanced adaptive techniques for managing emotions, including anger, fear, and frustration.

An additional research conducted by Fairleigh Dickinson University affirms that there is a positive correlation between children raised by authoritative parents and their academic performance. This may suggest that parents with an authoritative style of parenting tend to have a strong commitment to their children's development, establishing realistic objectives for them from an early stage.

As one would anticipate, in a household where clear parameters and regulations are established and adhered to, a probable outcome will be the occurrence of favorable conduct. Consider the situation from this perspective: prior to contravening the regulations, the children possess knowledge of the ensuing repercussions. They are confident that their parents will not exhibit leniency significant enough to grant them pardon. Moreover, these children possess a comprehensive understanding of the underlying reasons behind their parents' establishment of rules. Hence, adhering to regulations proves more facile in comparison to engaging in acts of defiance. This discipline strategy is formally referred to as inductive discipline. It encompasses the utilization of logical reasoning (induction) to elucidate the parents' actions, values, and disciplinary strategies.

Finally, as effective communication serves as the cornerstone in such households, children raised by authoritative parents frequently acquire adeptness in both communication and social abilities.

What are the drawbacks associated with adopting an authoritative parenting style?

As a parent who possesses authority, the task of establishing and consistently enforcing boundaries may require a substantial amount of forbearance and determination. Failing to implement these changes gradually can create significant stress for parents, thus becoming an onerous task.

Furthermore, in the event that this style of parenting is excessively practiced, the consequence could be an excessive proliferation of rules governing every element within your household. The residence ought to serve as an environment in which both you and your children derive pleasure. Nevertheless, when confronted with a constant barrage of regulations in every possible direction, your residence will inevitably transform into a source of dread, an outcome that you undoubtedly aim to avoid. The solution to this predicament lies in establishing a harmonious equilibrium between regulations and enjoyment. If a behavior does not have any adverse effects on your toddler's long-term development, it is appropriate to allow indulgence in enjoyable activities.

6. Hierarchical relationships

The ultimate factor contributing to anger in the workplace is the prevalent hierarchical organizational framework observed in nearly all businesses. In the context of hierarchical relationships, each ascending level exercises authority over the subordinate level. It is a common phenomenon for subordinate individuals to be vulnerable to the influence of their superiors, and it is not unusual for feelings of anger to arise within this dynamic.

This could be attributed to the lack of complete agency among subordinates regarding their sustenance, as they rely on employers for the necessary resources to financially support themselves. Authority figures wield significant influence over the tasks and methods employed by their subordinates, engendering a vulnerability in many individuals to experience apprehension. The convergence of fear and a diminished sense of agency frequently results in the intensification of anger, particularly in instances where those in positions of authority misuse their power or exhibit disrespectful behavior towards those under their command.

Choose every course of action that supervisors may employ in order to gain further understanding regarding its potential to incite anger within hierarchical dynamics.

Abuse their power

Individuals who hold positions of power or authority may experience a compelling urge to validate or assert their position by manifesting feelings of anger. This misuse of authority is expected to provoke resentment among the subordinate individuals. Conversely, in the event that a superior's power or authority is questioned, it is probable that the superior will become infuriated.

Treat subordinates with disrespect

In spite of the relationship between the parties involved, disrespect frequently serves as a catalyst for anger. When superiors exhibit disrespectful behavior towards their subordinates, it is reasonable to anticipate reciprocation in the form of anger. This can also be conveyed in a more nuanced manner, such as through counterproductive work behaviors.

Common Causes of Anger

Objectives: Utilize this employment resource to ascertain prevailing factors contributing to feelings of anger.

Having an understanding of the common factors that often provoke individuals' anger in a professional setting will enhance your comprehension of both your own frustrations and those experienced by your colleagues.

Research has indicated that there are five prevalent factors that contribute to anger in the workplace.

Common Causes of Anger

Displeasure with the system indicates that the functioning of your organization is not aligned with optimal standards, potentially leading to hindrances in productivity and fostering sentiments of frustration. Three common elements that contribute to dissatisfaction with the system and incite feelings of anger encompass heightened competition, organizational scale, and elevated performance demands.

Disparity in treatment Elicits displeasure among individuals, as they perceive others to be advantaged in the exchange dynamics. This implies that they hold the belief that an individual is receiving greater compensation with less exertion or input than they are.

Impeded objectives are a catalyst for frustration as the attainment of goals serves as a yardstick for professional accomplishment.

Divergent principles: When universally embraced work principles, such as industriousness, aptitude, and ethics, are met with disrespect or negligence, it has the potential to evoke feelings of anger.

Hierarchical relationships can evoke feelings of anger, particularly when individuals in positions of authority demonstrate a lack of respect or misuse their power when interacting with subordinates.

Consider this example. Dexter, an individual possessing expertise in graphic design, has recently reached an agreement to occupy a position within a diminutive advertising organization. He is experiencing a growing sense of dissatisfaction towards his job and harboring increasing resentment towards his boss. Please observe as Dexter elucidates his emotions.

Why does she consistently assign me tasks of low significance? I have the potential to achieve a higher level of productivity. Given the current pace, I am concerned about the lack of opportunities to gain valuable experience, which may hinder my professional growth.

May I inquire about the incident that occurred recently? When she jovially reminded me of the approaching performance evaluation? Was it a threat? Is this a admonition to modify my behavior? Alternatively, could this be interpreted as a manner of indicating that my employment is being terminated?

Dexter is worried.

Dexter lacks autonomy in his professional pursuits and is dissatisfied with the trajectory his career is currently following under the direction of his superior. He perceived her laughter, in the context of discussing his performance evaluation, as disconcerting and somewhat disrespectful. He is additionally concerned and apprehensive about the possibility of his boss delivering unfavorable news during this performance evaluation. The confluence of his inadequate restraint and apprehension has engendered resentment aimed at his superior.

Control

The perception of being under the control or influence of another entity can give rise to sentiments of resentment and belligerence. It is imperative to experience a sense of personal agency, where we perceive ourselves as the architects of our own destinies, independent from external influences or circumstances. Although our level of maturity has reached a point where we comprehend the importance of compromise and collaboration, we experience a sense of insufficiency when individuals consistently make all decisions on our behalf or present frequent unreasonable demands that we feel compelled to fulfill, whether it pertains to our personal lives, professional endeavors, or social interactions.

There exist three fundamental rationales accounting for the frequent experience of being subjected to control. Initially, although the concept of uniqueness is widely recognized as a significant ideal, individuals tend to concurrently desire adherence to well-established and familiar norms regarding appearance, personality, cognition, and lifestyle.

There is an expectation for conformity when it comes to our marital unions, physical appearances, and professional pursuits. When we deviate from the prevailing consensus, we frequently experience an inclination to realign ourselves with the normative group, and these mechanisms of conformity can be exasperating.

Additionally, there exists a prevailing anticipation for us to demonstrate a prescribed manner of behavior, and it appears as though each individual has devised their own strategy for our path. We may even actively seek out an individual to engage in dialogue regarding a matter; however, once they commence formulating a course of action for us to address said matter, we experience feelings of irritation and hostility.

We may desire an attentive audience to acquaint them with the account of how an unforeseen event disrupted our agenda for the day, yet we were not soliciting their advisement on improving our planning skills for the future. We may have disclosed to a friend our inability to promptly settle the electricity invoice due to an unforeseen expenditure; however, we did not anticipate them making the suggestion that acquiring a credit card and proactively saving for unforeseen circumstances would be a viable solution. Although these responses may appear innocuous, we did not solicit them as they impart a sense of judgment and control, oftentimes provoking feelings of anger within us.

Furthermore, we are burdened with a sense of duty to undertake tasks that have ceased to be voluntary. Our progenitor might instruct us that it is incumbent upon us to engage in scholastic pursuits upon our arrival at home, rather than indulging in video games for a singular hour post an arduous day of educational endeavors. Our spouse may express that dedicating time to our children immediately after work is a responsibility intrinsic to being a responsible parent. A companion frequently contacts us on a regular basis with various concerns she wishes to discuss, and we feel compelled to lend our attention.

It is imperative that individuals possess the liberty to compose their own compendiums on leading a fulfilling existence unburdened by obligatory commitments. The imposition of external regulations upon us evokes a sense of being constrained, leading to emotional distress. The subsequent explores the establishment of boundaries and the reduction of influence exerted by others, which is the recommended course of action in such circumstances. We should consistently uphold our freedom from external influence, and even though we may occasionally make poor choices, it is an inherent aspect of autonomy and a personal entitlement that remains unclaimed by others.

Reduce Your Stress

Frequently, various stimuli, actions, and circumstances elicit feelings of anger within you due to an elevated state of stress. In times of heightened stress, even the smallest incidents can provoke agitation, potentially culminating in an outburst of anger. In order to mitigate this issue, proactively address and manage your stress in a timely manner.

On occasions when you experience feelings of unease, disturbance, or frustration, center your attention on those emotions and endeavor to discern their underlying causes. If your stress stems from work-related challenges or an excessive workload, it may be beneficial to address these concerns with your supervisor, particularly if you perceive inequitable treatment towards you. If you are a business owner, endeavor to restrict your working hours and refrain from bringing work to your place of residence, ensuring that your time at home is solely dedicated to relaxation and rejuvenation. If your stress is attributed to a deficit in personal development, allocate some time for introspection and endeavor to comprehend your aspirations and inherent meaning in life.

Moreover, cultivate the practice of engaging in a restorative activity daily, even if it is for a mere duration of 15 minutes. Allocate a portion of each day to engage in activities that promote self-care and tranquility, resulting in a profound sense of rejuvenation. Potential alternatives in a formal tone: 1. One could choose to engage in leisurely activities such as watching a show, reading a book, or taking a leisurely stroll. Alternatively, one could partake in activities that promote relaxation, such as listening to soothing music, indulging in a refreshing shower or a leisurely bath, or receiving a massage. Additionally, one could opt for therapeutic activities like baking or engaging in any other calming pursuit. 2. It is possible to engage in a variety of activities conducive to relaxation, such as viewing a show, immersing oneself in a literary work, or embarking on a leisurely walk. Alternatively, one can choose activities that facilitate tranquility, like listening to melodies that soothe the senses, enjoying a revitalizing shower or a prolonged bath, receiving a therapeutic massage, creating culinary delights through baking, or embracing any other undertaking that yields a tranquilizing effect. 3. One has the option to partake in a range of activities that foster a sense of relaxation and well-being. These could include watching an entertaining show, immersing oneself in a compelling book, or embarking on a peaceful walk. Furthermore, one can opt for endeavors that promote serenity, such as indulging in calming music, embracing the restorative effects of a leisurely shower or a prolonged bath, seeking solace in a rejuvenating massage, engaging in the art of baking, or exploring alternative tranquilizing pursuits. As you gradually attend to your normal stressors, you will observe a noteworthy enhancement in your capacity to regulate various emotions, even those of high intensity and intricacy, such as anger. As your stress levels diminish, you will no longer experience agitation in response to unforeseen circumstances in your life; consequently, your anger will recede as your capacity to manage all emotions enhances.

Incorporating these strategies will assist in attaining a calm state whenever an overwhelming sense of anger is perceived. In order to further advance and enhance one's abilities as an emotional manager, it is advisable to cultivate a heightened sense of mindfulness towards one's emotions, particularly when it comes to anger. Demonstrating profound reverence towards anger, engaging in meditation practices, and embracing the virtue of forgiveness and letting go are all integral aspects of this journey.

The subsequent expounds upon these methodologies.

www.ingramcontent.com/pod-product-compliance
Lightning Source LLC
Chambersburg PA
CBHW052136110526
44591CB00012B/1742